The Knowledge of Good and Mostly Evil

Jonathan Edwards J. Olabre
August, 2019

Published and printed

by **TATAY JOBO ELIZES.**
Self-Publisher
in 2019, under the
permission and authorization
of **JONATHAN EDWARDS J. OLABRE**,
author and owner of the copyright to this book. The
copyright owner can withdraw this permission at his
discretion without any objection from Talay Jobo
Elizes at any time. Printing of this book is using the
present day method of Print-On-Demand (POD)
system, where prints will never run out of copies to
be available for posterity. The copyright owner is free
to republish with other publishers anytime.

KDP ISBN - 9781087284125
Independently Published

Contact: job_elizes@yahoo.com
jonedwards.olabre@gmail.com
Website: http://tinyurl.com/mj76ccq

About the author

Jonathan Edwards J. Olabre
(From his facebook profile)

Today is my birthday. Dec. 18, 2017

    I will greet you all this time around. To all of those who are part of my life, my brother and sisters, my nieces and nephews, my uncles and aunts, cousins. To all my friends whom I have known from childhood, grade school, high school, college and in the course of my professional life up to today. To neighbors, team mates and colleagues who have taught me all that I know. To all the people whom I have interacted with that included teachers and professors. I mention those who have also served as mentors, even former and present bosses at work that have taught me my life skills today. I greet all my brothers and sisters in the faith, never shall we be alone for God is with us always. Greetings to the Special Interest Groups that I belong to, from the political to the Geek

Sites and Groups. The Meek and the Geek shall inherit the earth.

Of course, to all past loves. Please forgive me for not mentioning your names Hahahahaha. No rancor or bitterness. I still love all of you and you remain in my heart.

To all of you, thank you very much. It has been 52 years and I have no regrets. The best part of the journey is getting to know all of you. You are all my treasures. I will always be grateful.

I started my day by going to the nearest church where I live. I am a Protestant but the nearest church is Roman Catholic. But God goes to where one seeks Him. I just gave thanks for everything and asked for nothing. I also went to the ossuary where the remains of Mama and Papa are relinquished. I prayed to God to convey to them how we are very thankful for them, how we miss them and how our love for them has never faded.

I gifted myself by having free lugaw meals be given to the street children, the beggars and the destitute courtesy of Alex Lugawan. Perhaps, God willing, it will be steak dinner for them next year.

Again, I send my greetings and felicitations to all of you. Thank you very much!

ooooo

Contents

ooooo

1

When We Were Punks
August 7, 2017

It was a typical Sunday afternoon. Mama, standing up after watching Lovingly Yours, Helen to prepare merienda. I was just waiting for the sun to go down enough so I can play basketball without being scorched. Looking out from the window of our unit, I saw Mr. Perez talking with other members of the Bagong Lipunan Community Association (BLCA). But there was something amiss. It was not the usual banter of neighbors and friends. They were talking as if in whispers and eyes cast furtively on either side. I went to my room and listened to my U2 tape. Then in the middle of Bono's voice singing Sunday Bloody Sunday, a knock on the door. I peeped out from my room's door and saw Lola Engga come in, but she talked with my mom, also in whispers.

It was August 21, 1983.

I knew Ninoy was coming home, but I didn't know it was to be that day. Days before I saw the yellow ribbons tied along parts of EDSA.

I heard it from an uncle and drew whatever information about it from the Marcos newspapers. The significance I knew little about. I remember Ninoy from a telecast way back in 1978. Followed by a noise barrage. But now, being a freshman in college that seemed to be an eternity ago.

"He was shot!", "They killed him!" That was what Lola Engga told my mother. Immediately after that, Mama enforced a lock down. All five of us, my sisters and brother were not allowed to go out. We tried watching TV but around 6:00 pm, there was a brownout. Nothing to do and nothing to watch. All we could do was watch from our windows and look at the darkness that descended. What we didn't fully realize was that a different and sinister darkness was already enveloping the land since 1972. We waited for electricity to return, but it didn't get restored that night.

Little did I know that the world has taken a turn, things are happening that affects me even to this day.

It was August 21, 1983.

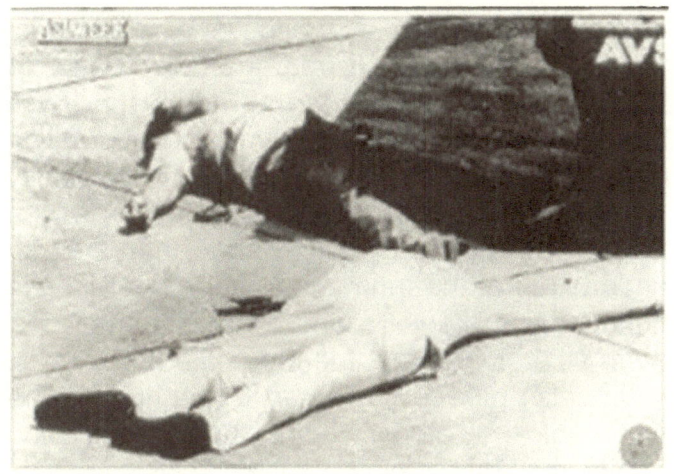

ooooo

2
Kian Sleeps with the Angels Now
August 18, 2017

"Now I am become Death, the Destroyer of Worlds" – Lord Krishna

The above quote was what I gave my brother for his essay when he was about to take the entrance exams for the Ateneo de Manila University decades back. My mother told me to help with the essay of my brother. It was about the power of man to do good or evil. It was uttered by Lord Krishna to Prince Arjuna while serving as the charioteer when they were facing an army composed of friends and relatives of the prince. Yes, I got it from the Bhagavad-Gita that my grandfather made me read when I was in 6th Grade. Lord Krishna was the incarnation of the Hindu god Vishnu. Faced with the reality of the moment, Lord Krishna told Prince Arjuna that it was "holy duty" or Dharma that is to be undertaken at the moment. In gung ho parlance during my military training days, it meant "Kill them all. Let God sort them out later!!" And yes, it was also uttered by Robert Oppenheimer, the father of the atomic bomb upon witnessing Trinity, the first atomic bomb test in New Mexico, USA.

I never knew it would haunt me back decades later. Last February 2017, I had to run after my niece who suddenly took off to take pictures during the EDSA Revolution anniversary. She was born in 1993 and never had any experience with the dangers of state sponsored murder. It was not like before during the rallies against the Marcos dictatorship when there was always a buddy system and we knew where to run in cases that abductions and dispersals were being conducted during the "mobs." I had to run after her and admonish her to never do that again. The times have changed and a murderous president was now the leader in this country. She never knew the terror of those days and had a default thinking that she was safe.

Kian also felt safe. He also never knew oppression and terror caused by government and state sponsored murder. He was 17 and at Grade 11. OPLAN Galugad was being undertaken in their community. It was not different from the "sona" during the Martial Law of Marcos. It always targeted the communities of the poor. It was made to appear that he fought back with a .45 caliber pistol. That is not what the CCTV footages recorded and not what the witnesses saw. It was plain cold blooded murder by agents of the state.

The tragedy is that many applaud the Philippine version of the "Night of the Long Knives" that was undertaken during the last few days. 32 in Bulacan, 26 in Manila and 18 in the KaMaNaVa area. They wanted to beat the record of having more deaths than in Ozamiz. It is an obscene game, a scoring contest that was being conducted as a competition of one up-manship by an institution that was supposed to protect the Filipino. Many clapped their hands and yet they are themselves saying that there is no slaughter. As Mocha would attest, they do shows every night and they see no slaughter in the streets.

To those who applaud, does Kian's death make you feel more secure? Does his death justify your frustrations with regards to your issues of traffic, late license plates and even long lines in the MRT? Has it reduced the price of rice to 15 pesos per kilo? Does Kian's death bring food to your tables? Does it give your children free education? Has that death made this country self-sufficient in rice? Has it ended corruption in government? Did it generate more jobs? Did it give free hospitalization and medicines? But it made you feel better didn't it? Satisfied your weekly quota for blood didn't it? Made you feel good because you have your own shortcomings. Made you feel strong and secure I am sure. Made you feel that the country is doing good by the number of deaths recorded.

But how come you don't do the killings yourself? You can't because you are all cowards and depraved. You put your frustrations on people who cannot defend themselves. You elect a leader who has no moral compunctions because he himself is depraved.

Last time I checked, that is called evil.

Tonight, Kian sleeps with the angels.

Kian, is just one and is now listed as a statistic to this silent holocaust of the Filipinos. It was also an August when depravity reigned and showed the utter depths that evil is willing to go.

August 21, 1983.

Every night will have its dawn. It is darkest now and it may even get darker. It will not last forever. It did not then, it will not now.

Then we will know Dharma. Then we will know who will become Death and the Destroyer of Worlds.

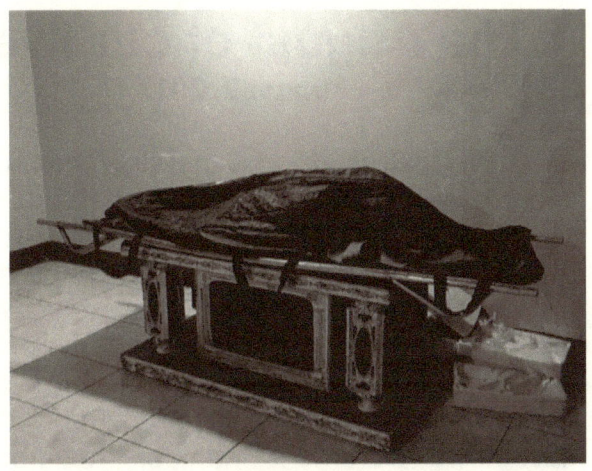

Kian Delos Santos, 17

AYON SA PULIS
Nung nakita kami, tumakbo. Nagpaputok.
Kaya napilitan kaming magpaputok.
Tinamaan. Patay. May 2 sachet ng Shabu.

ooooo

3

The August of our lives
August 2, 2017

August used to be the sixth month of the year, thus its name of Sixtilis, then February and March were added. Julius Ceasar named it August after Augustus, to commemorate most of his victories achieved during that month. August means respected and impressive. That is why The Senate was always referred to as the "August Chamber," but judging from what we have now, "Excrement Chamber" would be more apt.

In my youth, August was special. It was the birthday month of my sister Minnie who came after me. It was during her birthdays that the rains would not seem to cease. Almost always, by the time her birthday party ends, the floods start to rise. It meant no school and playing in the flood waters.

But the month of August had another effect later on with our lives. We lived in a government housing project then. We were trained and inculcated in the virtues of the New Society. Being members of the Kabataang Bagong Lipunan Tungo sa Kaunlaran (KABALIKAT) we not only had the best sports training but also comprehensive courses in arts and culture ranging from theater arts to museum excursions and art appreciation.

But it was in August 1983, I was in college when I saw yellow ribbons tied to posts and even pedestrian overpasses in EDSA. Ninoy was coming home.

It was 5 years since 1978 when I last saw Ninoy on TV during his one chance to campaign for the Interim Batasang Pambansa elections. His performance was scintillating and after that we knew that he would be cheated. A noise barrage was organized. Media was muzzled and information was passed via small paper notes. I remember riding my bike past Metrocom and PC checkpoints to deliver the messages to those who would participate. At the appointed time, Metro Manila erupted in noise. The Marcoses, who before that were comfortably ensconced in their seats of power were caught by surprise. They were surprised that a nascent opposition that was community-based was already existing. But they were still too strong. It was like the 1968 Prague Spring.

But on that fateful Sunday of August 1983, the cracks became fissures and the fissures became chasms. It was not only about Ninoy and the Aquinos, it was about a country held in the vise of oppression that discovered that fear is no obstacle to freedom. By that time it was all downhill for the dictatorship. Many lives were sacrificed but there was no preventing and avoiding the logical conclusion of 1986. One way or another, Marcos was finished.

We attained freedom but not in the absolute sense of the word. There was still poverty, hunger, hardships, problems, difficulties and the same system where the elite held political and economic power. But the gain was that we can already speak our minds. The real victory was that we can dream of a better country, a country that is free.

Another August in 2009, and the President who took over in 1986 passed away. Cory was never perfect, I did not agree with her when she wanted the US Bases to remain. But I was able to pursue my dreams in relative freedom. I never got rich but I was free and alive. Nobody hunted me for speaking my mind. And in that August, when she passed away, my family and other friends were in tears. How does one reward a person who was instrumental in freedom regained? By voting for her son Noynoy?

My vote was not about Necropolitics. Cory's death reminded me that even though Cory never completed the revolution, it was up to us Filipinos to work for its completion. No matter how hard, frustrating and difficult we must carry on. Never to compromise a false sense of security, conveniences and even rice for the freedom won at so much cost.

It is August 2017, dark clouds loom over the horizon. Things may seem futile at the moment but I see the Augusts of long ago, I think the same as Julius Ceasar, Augusts are the months of our country's greatest triumphs. The yellow Ribbons hang in our minds and hearts. This too will pass and our country will only come out so much stronger after this storm. God has never failed the faithful.

ooooo

4
Hate and Justice
Dateline, 2017

Hate and Justice

I was an elementary school student then and after doing my homework and dinner, I would go to my grandfather and watch him stack his books and Bible on the dining table. To the smell of katol, he would read and write to compose his Sunday sermon at church. It took him a few nights to draft, revise and finish his sermon. Sermons at Protestant Sunday Services would last at least an hour back then. Now they just want it short and sweet. But I digress. I would ask so many questions ranging from English subjects, mathematics, science, news that I read on the newspapers all the way to the American era that he grew up in. I would ask what they did since there was no electricity, the games they played and his playmates.

He told me of a playmate, a girl, his neighbor whose parents were Chinese. He told me of how pretty she was and how they were close friends. Tatay (that was how we called our grandfather) did not yet have his brother, Tiyo Bayani as a playmate. They were born 9 years apart. So this girl was his only playmate. Being children that they were, they often would lose track of time while playing. As in such cases, the father of the girl would get angry and punish the girl. Tatay told me how every time it happened she was beaten with a cane. Tatay would tell me how he heard every whoosh of the cane before it struck his playmate on the back, buttocks and legs. The girl never cried out according to Tatay. Tatay would feel the guilt of having been at fault because he felt guilty for playing so late in the day with the girl. Tatay would sit by the window and clench his fists and tremble for every whoosh he would hear. With this story unfolding before me, I also felt anger and rage. I could see his impassive face while he was telling me the story. He told me that his father, my great grandfather, Lolo Pedrito (or Pedrong Paos) to the neighbors, would just put both his hands on Tatay's shoulders to steady him. Lolo Pedrito will not say anything. Just firm hands on Tatay's shoulders. I asked Tatay what it was like to be a witness to such cruelty, to such punishment for so small an infraction? He just told me that he always found his playmate cheerful the next day and then they would play as if nothing had happened the night before. I asked if he was angry and he told me yes he was angry but what surprised me was that he did not have any hate for the father. Tatay told me that the hands on his shoulders were there to steady him, to show that there are things that happen in the world that we cannot control but must have the courage to face no matter how bad it seems. That was why he would play again the next day with his neighbor. He told me he always paid due courtesy to the parents of his playmate. One time, Lolo Pedrito told him "maaaring magalit ngunit walang pagka-muhi.". It is alright to feel anger but never hate. It was the same lesson that my grandfather told me although indirectly that night. Tatay lived on to survive WWII (almost executed by the Japanese on suspicions of being a guerilla) and the tumultuous years of Martial Law. I found him always taking on principled stands with regards to Martial Law. He was old by then but never lot the resolve for talking and discussing what is right and wrong to the chagrin of my uncle who was close to President Marcos.

Why do I tell this? This is why. I came across a column of Contreras that is trying to revise history just for the sake of being "fair" and that history of the Martial Law regime was based on "Hatred". With the death of 5 victims of EJK a block from where I live, I decided to fight back against this Cult of Death and Tyranny being espoused by this professor and columnist.

I will answer it point by point. Italics will be my riposte.

Contreras stated:

IT is wrong to deny the existence of the innocent casualties of martial law.

But it is equally wrong to treat as innocent victims those who by choice took up arms and embraced the communist ideology. They are rebels with a cause, and are in fact freedom fighters. To label them innocent victims is to insult the virtue and the power of their politics.

I say:

Those who took up arms against the dictatorship never professed innocence in the middle of a firefight. It was never heard in the middle of the battle that troops should stop firing since the NPAs were "innocents". I challenge that any after action report be submitted that there were such things. In the event of GRP victories, I have yet to come to read such a report. In cases of NPA victories, there was nary a remark of such tactics.

But I point out to documented evidence that is now at the Human Rights Victims Claims Board that no combatans filed for compensation because they were killed or injured in a firefight. In fact, those huge piles of documents told of imprisonment, torture and death not from firefights.

Contreras says:

These were young students who saw hope in the leftist ideology, urban workers who were politicized by the exploitative working conditions that their capitalist masters inflicted on them, and rural peasants who were in search of liberation from bondage by their oppressive landlords. Their politics is one driven by a revolutionary struggle, and one that they deliberately chose.

I say:

Students who saw hope in leftist ideology? Edgar Jopson was laughed at by the more radical students who belonged to the Kabataang Makabayan (KM) since he was a burgis and malabnaw. He was never a member of KM but of the moderate National Union of Students of the Philippines (NUSP). In fact he was from the Ateneo then, one of two most elitist schools in the Philippines, the other one was De Lasalle College. The other fact is that Marcos himself considered the NUSP as moderate in its stances that he even acceded to an audience with the NUSP leaders. When Edgar Jopson asked that Marcos put in writing that he will not run or aspire for a for a third term (the 1935 Constitution barred any president from a third term), Marcos was livid and remarked "why should I treat with the son of a grocer?" and "why should I listen to them, their English is not even elegant." With such treatment and by declaring Martial Law, I know asked who put the students towards the fold of the only alternative left at that time? When Martial Law was declared, these students and their leaders were rounded up and those who managed to escape the dragnet were driven to the only remaining alternative remaining. Congress was padlocked, The Supreme Court were composed of 9 Marcos appointees out of eleven and the Press was muzzled. What would you have those students do? Join the Mickey Mouse Club?

The workers? Most industries were then controlled by the oligarchy. But then, Marcos was funded in the 1965 Elections by the oligarchy. In fact, the Lopez business empire funded Marcos against Macapagal. The 1969 elections were also funded by the oligarchy. So, who was in any position to stand up for the workers? Philippine industry was in the stranglehold of US business interests at that time. Who else would have the capacity for manufacturing and even agriculture after WWII? Ever heard of Parity Rights? The Laurel-Langley Act gave a sunset provision on it that it would end in 1973. But Marcos using Martial Law extended it for another year. Marcos used the excuse that nationalist economic policies were being espoused by the demonstrators so as that why he also declared Martial Law. This Marcos told to US Ambassador Byroad.

Filipino workers were exploited to the hilt. In fact there was no 60/40 Filipino/Foreigner limit that time. Even in the early 80s, Filipino workers in Mattel, Parke-Davis and Stanford Microsystems were subject to oppression from management and further oppression from the apparatus of Martial Law when it came to fighting for their rights and better compensation. Their leaders were arrested and their picketlines were assaulted and dispersed.

Marcos boasted to potential investors that strikes were prohibited because of Martial Law. If you were a worker then, were would you come to for redress? Marcos drove labor to the left.

Farmers? The 40 days and nights of rain in 1970 brought out the worst flooding in Central Luzon for decades. Central Luzon was considered the Rice Granary of the country. This resulted in rice shortages that extended all the way to 1973. So those who say that the country was self-sufficient in rice during the time of Marcos are on Fentanyl. The only time was in 1977 when there was a chance to export rice but not in big volumes.

The floods during that time so affected the rice farmers. During the flood itself many were just on rooftops while the only idea of Disaster Risk Reduction and Management was footages of the First Lady throwing plastic bags of Nutribuns from Huey Helicopters to families on rooftops. It never occurred that drinking water was also needed. The devastation was so wide that months after the floods, relief and rehabilitation was being conducted. Students from Manila went to the countryside to help in the effort. That was when the students saw the deplorable conditions of the farmers flood or no flood. These students experienced what it was to be a farmer, they told their immersion to fellow students. That was another factor for the rise of student activism. Students saw with their own eyes that there was a malaise. The farmers have nobody and nowhere to turn to. Aside from the generations old tenancies they have no assistance from government.

Declaring Land Reform in 1973 did not solve the problems. The law had conditions that enabled big land holders to retain their landholdings. Why? Marcos was still of the mind that Martial Law was still unstable and that he needed the support of large landlords or else they would gang up on him if he defied them. The farmers had nobody to turn to. Guess who drove them to the arms NPA?

From a strength of 800 at the declaration Martial Law in 1972, the NPA had at its peak at 26,000 by 1986 before Marcos fled.

Contreras said:

However, theirs are only some of the many political narratives that populated the Marcos years.

There is also the narrative of the state, as an institution that has a right to protect itself from any threat, and in fact has the monopoly of the legitimate use of political violence, only restrained by its commitment to civilized rules of engagement. The burden was for the state to justify its use of violence in accordance with the law. Declaring martial law suspends some rights, but it does not give the state the freedom to kill without justification. Even in war there are rules.

I say:

What were the reasons for Martial Law? What justified it? If we go by the reasons of Marcos such as the NPAs, lawlessness, economic collapse and social decadence, then I answer initially not from a subjective point of view but from a documented source that has institutional credibility until this very day.

There was nothing in the Philippine situation that would have generated panic or hysteria. Just a year before the imposition of martial law, the prestigious Rand Corporation surveyed the Philippine situation on commission from the U.S. Agency for International Development. The Rand report underscored among others the fact that:

1. "The political system appears to be stable and generally responsive to the desire of most people."

2. "The economy appears to be performing better than commonly thought and is spread broadly across the country."

3. "Crime is not a national problem. Violence and fear of violence are concentrated in a few areas."

4. "The HMB (Hukbong Mapagpalaya ng Bayan or NPA) are not a serious threat to the government."

So what in the name of Sam Hill would Marcos declare Martial Law for when even the most Rightist and Conservative Think Tank at that time said there were no reasons to do so?

My gin is almost consumed. I will continue with this tomorrow.

Bilog lang pala katapat mo Contreras!

Hate and Justice Part II

As for Rights that some were only suspended and not all, I beg to differ since freedom and liberty are all the most fundamental of Rights. The fact that the Supreme Court that encompasses the Judiciary was itself defanged:

"I do hereby (further) order that the Judiciary shall continue to function in accordance with its present organization and personnel, and shall try and decide in accordance with existing laws all criminal and civil cases, except the following :

1. Those involving the validity, legality or constitutionality of Proclamation No. 1081, dated September 21,1972, or of any decree, order or acts issued, promulgated or performed by me or by my duly designated representative pursuant thereto.

2. Those involving the validity, legality or constitutionality of any rules, orders or acts issued, promulgated or performed by public servants pursuant to decrees, orders, rules and regulations issued and promulgated by me or by my duly designated representative x x x"

What Rights remain after these?

1) Shutdown of, and imposition of government control over, all media and other means of giving out information;

2) Arrest and detention, in most cases without charges or complaint, of thousands allegedly involved, wittingly or unwittingly, in a conspiracy to overthrow the government.

3) Placing of all public utilities under military supervision;

4) Banning of mass action in rallies or demonstrations, of criticisms of public officials and of the inalienable right of workers to strike and picket.

5) Closing of all schools for one week. (Actually, it was a month. I remember)

6) Imposition of curfew from 12 o'clock midnight to 4 o'clock in the morning, reduced later to from 1 o'clock in the morning to 4 o'clock in the morning.

7) Carrying of firearms outside residence without the permission of the armed forces of the Philippines became punishable by death.

8) Suspension of the departure of Filipinos abroad, except on official mission.

The reason Martial Law was declared was because Democracy was starting to work as evidenced by protests borne out of the grievances by the poor and marginalized. These then put pressure on institutions that were designed to address such in the first place. That the pressure was applied because of better organizing and conveyance of messages that have long been unheard and ignored.

Marcos used this as a picture that Democracy was in danger from the same people who wanted to benefit from the fruits of a real and responsive democracy.

But what did constitute the consolidation of the powers of the Executive, the Legislative and the Judiciary upon one man by virtue of the declaration of Martial Law by Marcos? Marcos usurped the powers of bot co-equal branches of government by issuing the following:

General Orders. This was for the Armed Forces of the Philippines (AFP). In General Order No. 1 which was dated September 22, 1972, "NOW, THEREFORE, I, Ferdinand E. Marcos, President of the Philippines, by virtue of the powers vested in me by the Constitution as Commander-in- Chief of the Armed Forces of the Philippines, do hereby proclaim that I shall govern the nation and direct the operation of the entire Government, including all its agencies and instrumentalities, in my capacity and shall exercise all the powers and prerogatives appurtenant and incident to my position as such Commander-in-Chief of all the armed forces of the Philippines, x x x"

This enabled Marcos to control not just the Executive Department but also those that composed local government units who were under the Civil Service and also those appointed by elected officials.

Letters of Instructions. This enabled Marcos to control the entire civil bureaucracy regardless of the Security of Tenure afforded by the rules and regulations of the Civil Service Commission.

Also, Marcos specifically barred the Judiciary from vital areas of judicial functions, notable among which was any case involving the validity, legality or constitutionality of Proclamation No. 1081 (the Declaration of Martial Law) itself and "any rules, orders or acts issued, promulgated or performed" by him or his duly authorized representatives.

Marcos also created Military Commissions or Tribunals to try civilian cases. Also, Letter of Instructions No. 11 that gave Marcos the power to remove members of the Judiciary at will and even without cause.

Upon the declaration of Martial Law, Marcos issued a Letter of Instructions to all government personnel that they tender their resignations. They were considered fired if Marcos accepts their letter of resignation. Thus, Marcos controlled everything and all rights were abolished. It is a lie that there were rights that were retained.

Contreras said:

There is a need to diligently account for every death, pain and suffering during martial law, if only to give us an accurate picture of how much of it was done in the context of legitimate political warfare between the state and the CPP-NPA-NDF, and how much of it was done in excess of such and were blatant forms of unwarranted political violence.

It is too simplistic to give a blanket label to all these deaths as unwarranted atrocities. The death of an unarmed civilian mistaken to be a communist sympathizer is different from the death of a communist guerrilla who died while engaging military forces. The death of a captured sympathizer who resisted arrest and was involved in a gunfight with his captors should be distinguished from someone who was tortured and executed by paramilitary or government forces while in custody.

The pain and suffering of students who chose to take up arms should not be dismissed as insignificant. But these should not be seen in the same way we see the pain and suffering of their families who were even harassed by agents of the state as a consequence of their choices.

The narratives of pain and suffering during the period of martial law are so complex that it is total historical irresponsibility to lump all of these as exhibits for the evil which was conveniently simplified as a Marcos monopoly.

I say:

Of course there is a need to diligently account for all the sins of Marcos and Martial Law. But not in the context of those who suffered, died and were imprisoned was because of the political warfare between the CPP/NPA/NDF.

In the 1946 Nuremberg Trials, Goering, Hess, Speer, Doenitz, von Runstedt and all the other German generals and Nazi Ministers all pled not guilty. But they were sentenced nonetheless because history, the outcome of the war was enough evidence that they were wrong. Was the Nuremburg Tribunal wrong when it ruled and gave a blanket label to all the atrocities committed? No. It was the right thing to do. We have yet to have such a tribunal but history is the ultimate tribunal. Now, there are efforts to change the tribunal or orient it to an obscene direction that totally turns a blind eye to what transpired during those dark years. If the Martial Law era was so complex, then WWII was even more complex but they (the Nuremberg Tribunal) made the correct decisions not based on nitpicking. To point out that there are details (numbers of killed, imprisoned tortured because of actual combat operations) have not been hashed out and that until we have the details then Martial Law was not so bad after all is the height of intellectual dishonesty.

Contreras said:

Professor Ambeth Ocampo, a noted historian, has virtually thrown a challenge to all of us, when he revealed the state of mind of Ninoy Aquino who, according to declassified US documents, insinuated some level of support for Marcos' decision to declare martial law. Even more interesting, Ocampo also revealed how Ninoy even had the musings of a dictator himself, when he intimated that if he were President, he would execute all corrupt officials.

I say:

Prof. Ambeth Ocampo quoted declassified US documents. That is well and good. But there are also documented evidence that Aquino defied the declaration of the coming Martial Law. He made that expose in the senate with his privilege speech about Oplan Sagittarius, the blue print for Martial Law. Unknown to Aquino, there was indeed a blue print but the name of the blue print was based according to the sources that Marcos gave the plans. So "Sagittarius" was assigned to only 1 general and then Marcos knew who the leaker was. In spy novel parlance, the assignment of coded names to each recipient of any plan was called a "Canary Trap". The general was marginalized after that.

But getting back to Aquino, then Manila Mayor Antonio Villegas told Ninoy to flee the Philippines since according to his US Intelligence "contacts", Marcos is set to declare Martial Law anytime soon. "But if Marcos declares martial law, he will have to get me within the first few hours, or he will never get me at all," Aquino restated a line he had given two days earlier to interviewers Marita and Jorge. Marita and Jorge were reporters of the Daily Express, a daily broadsheet ran by the brother of Imelda Marcos, Kokoy Romualdez. It was published in Daily Express.

There are also stories of how Aquino was warned by Enrile, Tatad and Col. Gatan (who eventually arrested Aquino) 40 minutes before the arresting party was to arrive. But Aquino still continued with is meetings with Sen. Tolentino, Sen. Padilla and others at the Hilton. He would get a phone call and then he would turn pale but after that return to his usual self. There were 3 phone calls. Then he called fellow senator into a bathroom and told him that Marcos just declared Martial Law and he will be arrested. He was arrested after that in the Hilton Hotel.

So, these documented stories, from a Marcos newspaper at that has more weight than declassified US documents. But again, why did Aquino kept harking on Oplan Sagittarius if he was in favor of Martial Law? Why does the sun rise in the east?

Contreras said:

It is narratives like these that force us to treat historical revisionism not as a revolting endeavor, but in fact as the preferred mode for researching and writing history. It is in being ready to objectively inquire into Ninoy and Marcos, and martial law, that we will be fair to our history.

A history that is blinded by hate will prevent us from having a total grasp of the complex events in our past. Consequently, it will constrain the healing of our nation's wounds and allow the self-interest of political elites to profit from it.

I say:

Where in the statements I wrote advocate hate with regards to the treatment of history? What I wrote gives the facts of what transpired in an Unknown History. It does not foment violence and hatred. In fact my intention was to give information on what transpired during that time. There are still stories to be told, many of them in the Human Rights Victims Claims Board being processed right now.

I go back to what I learned from my grandfather. If there is injustice, then rage against it. But most importantly try to find a solution. If nothing can be done about it at the moment, then make sure it never happens again.

The whoosh of the cane being heard before hitting the legs, buttocks and back of my grandfather's playmate more than 100 years ago is just like what the Filipinos felt during the height of Martial Law. There is anger but never turn it into hate. By hating we are no better than Marcos and his evil cabal. Of course evil must be fought on the beaches, the mountains, jungle fastness, in every village, city, road and if need be from house to house. But it is not done because of hate, it is because there must be justice. A justice based on those who prefer to be human even though it is seen as a weakness by an enemy that is unfettered by morals.

The real justice is that the whoosh of the cane be never heard ever again.

ooooo

5

In Blackest Day and Darkest Night
Dateline: Nov. 9, 2016

The Supreme Court Decision of 9-5 junking the petition against the burial of former President Ferdinand E. Marcos at the Libingan ng mga Bayani came as a shock to those who expected a ruling favoring the petition. Indignation was instantaneous and spontaneous. By late afternoon, demonstrations and rallies were being undertaken in various locations.

For me, I was born in 1965. It took a while for all of it to sink in. Although I was distraught because the decision, a certain paralysis overtook me a few hours later. I felt anger at first, I refused to post anything on my Facebook account, limiting myself to commenting on posts made by friends. I tried to make sense of it, trying to find that silver lining. I even tried to look at it as perhaps a sign from God.

At my age now, I have already thought of my "escape plan". That is a contingency plan when I eventually will retire. It was a plan to leave everything behind. Having read so many books on how to secure the retirement years and not be dependent on pensions. Yesterday, it seemed that I better have another plan.

I only have to look at the faces of my nieces and nephews in my mind's eye. I could never in my life leave them to what has just transpired. Even just after the elections, my siblings who had children would talk and say that everything they had worked for and sacrificed for the future came crashing down. They said that "Nai-panalo na naming dati ang kalayaan (We have already won freedom before)." Why should our children live in fear 30 years after?

As I was in those thoughts, it again drifted further back. It was a time that there was no TV, or radio or newspapers came out. I was still in Grade 1 then. But almost immediately I felt the change. We had no classes for 1 month. Then before going to school, my elders told me not to talk about Marcos. I come from a politically active family and I had a grand uncle who was a senator at that time. We always opposed Marcos.

I learned about the curfew, whenever I see the Metrocom patrol car coming down the street, it was time to go inside the compound gate. I worried about watching my mouth in school. After Lupang Hinirang we were made to sing The Bagong Lipunan March every day. Our Social Studies subject was changed into reading and studying Junior Citizen and Current Events Digest whose main contents were the projects and programs of the New Society. We never learned about Bonifacio, Rizal, Mabini, etc.

But etched in my mind forever is the "Sona" done to our neighborhood. When the Metrocom and PC would conduct saturation drives. All men would be told to come out into the street, take off their clothes and be subjected to searched. The Metrocom carried a list wherein names were announced and those who were in the list were carried off. I peeked in one of our Capiz windows which I bored a hole to watch from inside.

For a child, such memories of terror would never be erased. My terror is still inside my head even up to now. I knew it was wrong and dangerous to fight against the regime, but I also was able to put my licks in. In 1978, when the Noise Barrage was being organized, the only way to convey the messages was by passing a piece of paper with instructions. I rode my bicycle past the Metrocom and PC checkpoints to pass along the message. I just graduated Grade 6 then. I remember the scenes so vividly util now and they were made even more vivid with the SC decision yesterday. It is like a recurring nightmare and Freddy Kreuger just keeps on returning.

The terror of yesteryears are creeping back. The SC just made all the terror justified by its ruling. The person who enveloped the country in darkness decades ago was rewarded for the act. His family is rejoicing and basking in their regained legitimacy.

There is anger, indignation and gnashing of teeth by those who survived and fought the dictatorship. I was talking to a friend, she just told me "Wala naman tayong magagawa (We cannot do anything)". A pall has descended over this benighted land.

The sacrifices made years before seem to have been made in vain. It is easy now to just accept what has befallen our land and our people. But the memories that were rekindled yesterday would never permit me to just roll over and die. In fact, it has reactivated long dormant fires that were just embers the day before.

My face and those faces of my friends are now interspersed with the faces of my nieces and nephews. Now I understand. It was never for us, the torch we carry is for them. This time around, the light will not be so easily snuffed out.

We owe it to our heroes, martyrs and sacred dead. In this Darkest Day and Blackest night.We will not fail them.

ooooo

6
Hindi Ko Akalain
Jonathan Edwards J. Olabre   **38**

(Never Expected This)
October 13, 2016

(Chief Fun Officer at <u>Stark Industries</u> - Schools attended - Ama Computer College, Computer Science and Pio Del Pilar Educ. Instituion + Lives in Pasig City)

Hindi Ko Akalain.

It finally happened. Last night at around 7:00 PM, I have just finished dressing up. It was just to join school batchmates who were having a game of darts at the usual hangout. I was delayed from going out earlier since there was a thunderstorm. I had to take a bath and change clothes because I was caught in the rain on my way home. As I was picking up my things to bring, there were a series of loud raps on my door. As I opened it, there were 2 barangay tanods and 4 policemen. "28 B ba ito?" asked the tanod, I answered yes. I asked them who they were looking for, they did not answer but replied with "28 B ba ito?" I said yes again. Then they started looking furtively on all sides. I personally know the 2 tanod. And they also knew me. Then they retreated a few paces. I asked them again who were they looking for. No answer, then I told them if they needed anything. I told them that all the houses along this side are all numbered 28. They asked about 28 A, I told them where it is and I also told them that a city official lives there. Then they went away. I also went out and I saw them again. I asked again that if they needed anything from me since I am about to leave. They told me no, I was not needed.

I left but I no longer played darts. Between the laughing and the jokes and the ribbing from my batchmates that night, I was thinking. Was there Oplan Tokhang at night? The games ended and I went home. The morning after I was told that what happened was a mistake. There was a tip received yesterday that there was somebody taking shabu at an address and my address 28 B was given. It turned out that there was a mistake. It should have been 26 B.

Then it dawned on me. It was not Oplan Tokhang after all. It was a raid and my address was on the tip given by someone. It was a mistake but then the rage of all the things that transpired welled up in me. The thought of being a mistake, a collateral damage leaped from the newspaper headlines and right into my consciousness. It was me. I felt chills run up my spine and at the same time felt outrage. The cold arms of Death was wrapped around my shoulders the night before. They thought I was sniffing shabu. They received an unconfirmed tip that I was a drug addict. They went to my house, my house to see if I was sniffing shabu. Salpicas de mierda! Verdamt!

Only the 2 tanods saved me. They did not exactly say it but they recognized me. They know me. Then they realized that it was a mistake. It was that close! I was almost No. 3,001 on this days of terror. It was just a difference of 2 in that tipped off address. What if I had gone earlier? Would have they waited for me to go into that tipped off address and then what? What if it was a different tanod who accompanied the police? The vagaries of fate is what makes the difference then.

I ask my friends now who voted for Duterte. What would they say if the worst happened to me? "Jonathan was just collateral damage." "Oh it was a tragedy." Worse is "ah Jonathan used shabu. That is why he was so against Duterte." But you know me guys, I never touched the stuff.

The war has reached my front door. It is a war between good and evil. It is a war between civilization and barbarism. It is a war for our national soul. I just wonder when their eyes will open. Will I be just one of the casualties of this war?

I told a good friend about this earlier. She told me that I should keep quiet for the meantime with regards to my anti-Duterte posts. Ngayon pa ba ako tatahimik? I will not shut up. I will heighten my resistance. Writing this is part of that resistance. I will not be cowed. I will not be afraid because I am already terrified. Terrified on what has become of us. It was not like this a year ago. We have fought and won freedom 30 years ago. We defeated oppression 30 years ago. The War On Drugs is no longer abstract for me. I never knew we would come to this pass. Hindi Ko Akalain.

There is a storm coming and it is a storm that nobody has ever seen.

"A poet must also know how to lead an attack." – Ho Chi Minh

ooooo

7
Today is Wednesday Revisited
September 20, 2017

Wednesday is what most of us consider as the middle of the week. Something to look forward to at the end of the workday knowing that the other half of the week will lead to the weekend. It is a touchstone for most of the working class. It is as if the worst is now behind us. We can cruise until the weekend comes. Wednesday is the crossroads in the week. For those who have labored so hard on Monday and Tuesday. In most bars, Wednesday is Ladies' Night. A Promotion to lift up the spirits of the stressed and tired, to tide them over until the weekend. Days of recuperation and respite. A time for home, family and friends. A time for the weekly rewards.

Today is Wednesday because our country is stuck in the quagmire of a bloody Civil War in Marawi which is already going on for more than 100 days and no definite timetable to end the bloodbath. Today we have Filipinos fighting fellow Filipinos. A Secessionist movement borne out of the wrong decisions made by Marcos in settling the Mindanao Question. Of a Muslim populace already seething from the injustices experienced since colonial times. Of the Jabidah Massacre that prompted a mild mannered UP Professor to found the Moro National Liberation Front. It is still Wednesday today in Marawi. All those who perished, died on a Wednesday. The fighting continues all the day on Wednesday.

Today is Wednesday and the War Against Drugs continue. More than 13,000 dead and counting. Now they kill our young. Kian, Carlo, Kulot and many more. No death penalty law in the country and yet death is now the law.

Today is Wednesday. We have lost the West Philippine Sea to China in exchange for still unfulfilled railroads.

Today is Wednesday. Our democratic institutions are under siege. The Supreme Court, the Ombudsman. A House of Representatives and a Senate suborned by a president.

Today is Wednesday. The very fabric of morality and values are being shredded. There is no more civil discourse. There is only hate in social media. There is fake news and above all, a foul mouthed leader who curses everybody.

This Wednesday is also when many applaud uncouth behavior.

Today is Wednesday. The economy shows strength in GDP indicators and yet the poorest of the poor have yet to benefit from it. International Rating Agencies have yet to put food on the tables of millions of Filipino children who will sleep on mats, cardboards, bare floors and garbage without eating supper. Those who are sick will not get any doctors, medicines and medical attention today because is Wednesday. Many of them will die because they did not have the medicines and medical attention because it is Wednesday.

Today is Wednesday. Many of the people have no jobs because of failed economic policies made during that Wednesday. Industrialization was thrown out so as to assuage the IMF-WB conditions on what the Philippine economy must be after the 1947 Bretton Woods Agreement.

In exchange for loans, the country must not industrialize. our people will just be the market for the products of other countries. our people will just be hewers of wood and carriers of water.

And yet the country will need dollars to survive. Hotels, the Cultural Center, PICC, Folk Arts Theater, the Manila Film Center were financed by those loans in order to attract tourists. Agreements were made with Middle East countries for Philippine labor. At such a cost. The cost was a Presidential Decree,

PD1177 that automatically allocated 40% of Philippine government revenues to automatic debt payment. Now, no industrialization meant no jobs. Now we have the Diaspora of Filipinos to foreign lands. The cost is social and very hard to measure. The very fabric of the Filipino family is now being threatened. How I miss my sister and brother. These all happened on Wednesday.

Today is Wednesday. When elected and appointed government officials run roughshod over the people. Giving them crumbs, corrupting their values and morals so as to sustain a Ruling Class that is answerable to no one. Of having the biggest mansions, the most delicious food, the best and fanciest vehicles, the most lavish parties, the finest clothes and the most money. They do so because of the Pork Barrel system. They do so because of corruption. They do so because they have made beggars of the people so that they will be elected again and again and again.

Because it is always Wednesday and they made a Mendicant State.

Macliing Dulag. Dr. Johnny Escandor, Eman Lacaba, Edgar Jopson, Alex Boncayao, and thousands of soldiers, MNLF, NPA, activists, workers and way before them Elias, they all died on Wednesday.

It is a Wednesday today and tomorrow, shall our country be in a perpetual Wednesday?

Today is Wednesday. Our country is at the crossroads. We must decide if we are to be a better country, having ridden over the hump for the promise of a weekend or to be stuck on Wednesday.

All the evil started on Wednesday. In Malacanang. Marcos surrounded by his Rolex Twelve. They were making the countdown.

September 20, 1972 was a Wednesday. The next day was September 21, 1972. The day Martial Law was declared.

Today is a Wednesday.

Ooooo

8
I am Tired
Dateline, 2012

I wrote this 5 years ago when I still worked for government. I never knew it would get worse.

I Am Tired

I am tired. Tired of getting up each new day to go to work. Of undergoing the commute. Of the traffic And pollution. Of the threats of hold ups inside the FX.

I am tired of the inane babble that I hear on the radio being played inside the FX. Of balasubas and balahura. Of realizing how low the great number of our people can even identify themselves to those descriptions. On how low our values have sunk. Of a people willing to be described as such.

I am tired. Tired of putting my heart and soul into a job that is meant to save, uplift and educate such people. Of putting my neck on the line so as to be able to satisfy their needs. To solve their problems and to give comfort.

I am tired. Tired that inspite of what I do, I get brickbats, intrigue and false accusations. These come from people who would rather maintain the status quo so as to continue their making profit from the misery of others.

I am tired. Tired of taking the moral high ground when my enemies stoop to the lowest and most underhanded tactics to sow intrigue.

I am tired. Tired that those who only try to sow discord are the ones Seemingly invincible in their positions.

I am tired. Tired that those who do right are left twisting in the wind and those who do wrong are seen to prosper and thumb their noses at me.

I am tired. Tired that those who are in power choose to go the way of political expediency, realpolitik, of parochialism, and even school ties and family connections to snuff out righteous reforms.

I am tired. Tired of not trying to protect myself. Tired of betrayals and traitorous actions from people I trusted.

I am tired. Tired of understanding and rationalizing the actions of people who make things hard for those who wanted to do right.

I am tired. Tired of seeing people hungry for food.

I am tired. Tired of seeing people hungry for justice.

I am tired. Tired of seeing hardworking people not getting their rewards.

I am tired. Tired of believing a system wherein merit is not rewarded.

I am tired. Tired of all the hypocrisy of all our institutions.

I am tired. Tired of the apathy, the willingness and even support of a broken down system.

I am tired. Tired of the compromise to make what is good evil and what is evil right.

I am tired. So tired of the unwillingness of those who see the problem and yet refuse to point out that the Emperor has no clothes.

I am tired. Tired of seeing the sacrifices of those who came before us be unrecognized. Tired of statues of our heroes be covered by tarpaulins of those who cannot hold a candle to them.

I am tired but am unwilling to quit. to the very last breath, to the last iota of energy, to the last pulse, to the last drop of blood. Those of you who think you have won. My warning. There will come a time for accounting of all your sins. Laugh aloud now. Rejoice. me and my kind will show you the reverse of what you have done. With the help of Divine Providence, our iron will, we will win and we will prevail! The time will come when we will come for you. And by then, seek your peace with God.

ooooo

9
Every Morning
Dateline, 2017

"The real hopeless victims of mental illness are to be found among those who appear to be most normal. "Many of them are normal because they are so well adjusted to our mode of existence, because their human voice has been silenced so early in their lives, that they do not even struggle or suffer or develop symptoms as the neurotic does." They are normal not in what may be called the absolute sense of the word; they are normal only in relation to a profoundly abnormal society. Their perfect adjustment to that abnormal society is a measure of their mental sickness. These millions of abnormally normal people, living without fuss in a society to which, if they were fully human beings, they ought not to be adjusted."

— Aldous Huxley, Brave New World Revisited

"Tralala, tweedlededeedee it gives me a thrill, to wake up in the morning and hear the mockingbirds trill…" I heard that song when I was very young. It was being played on the radio when my grandparents were listening while having breakfast. With Milo and pan de sal with spiced ham it made my morning. Those days are gone.

I have had that feeling of an attack from an unexpected source since Grade 5. I felt it at school. I have classmates and teachers who I remember so well and never was I a victim of bullying. It was just the usual roughhousing in an all-boys school ran by priests. The stern teachers were strict but nurturing. At home, it was ideal as can be under any circumstances. A tall, providing father, a caring and kind mother, solicitous sisters a beloved little brother and loving grandparents were the environment. I have friends I the neighborhood and their parents were also friends of my parents.

But even though I did good in school, those mornings were started with feelings of dread that I cannot understand why there was that feeling. I buried myself in books and biking. The feeling never went away though. I fact, it went to a point where I did not want good things to happen because I knew bad things will happen just to take away happiness.

Such was the state of things that I thought was normal even in high school. I learned to deal with it never expected anything happy to happen or never wanted it to happen since there will come a day of gloom to take it all away.

The Knowledge of Good and Mostly Evil

With the way things went in the world, I thought it was normal. I thought it was just the way the world is. But I remember days when I was paralyzed by it. Days when I did not want to go to school or days I did not want to go to work even though I was doing good than many.

In college, the day started with Valium 10 that was supplied by a childhood friend because we thought it was cool and after the 1st class, my college buddy who is my lifelong best friend until now would tell me to start drinking Rhum Coke. He would have this 1 liter bottle of Coke which was half filled with Tanduay and of course the guards in the school thought it was only Coke. We studied and passed subjects and even got high grades in Physics at that. It was a coping mechanism. The College Guidance Counselor and the Office of Student Affairs identified me and my buddy and subjected us to a psycho test. It turned out that we were both neurotic and we laughed at it. They said they wanted us to take the test because we looked "weird." Years later I saw the former Director of the Office of Student Affairs and he told my boss (I was already working for the palace then) that I was one of the leaders of the "counter-culture" during college.

But that was after I was subjected to psychiatric care. I was diagnosed with clinical depression. My former boss tricked me into going to a psychiatric clinic because I was really spaced out. I was good at work, in fact, I was excelling at work. But by then, after work, my boss and I would go out for drinks after work and I can consume 20 bottles of beer without getting drunk. My former boss was worried and it turned out that the depressant in alcohol cannot go down to the level of depression that my system was already in. My system was already depressed. I was given medications and counseling. Eventually, I pulled back from the brink. But it never really went away.

Such that every morning, I would wonder why I am still alive and I have to explain and rationalize to myself that I have to live for that day. Every sunset that I see, I would have to explain to myself why I should not also end it that time.

I may be in Megamall and yet feel alone. I may be at the grand lobby of a hotel during a meeting and I would see everything spinning around me. Then it would be an anxiety attack and I would break out in cold sweat, shiver, tremble and feel like throwing up. It gets worse if I have had a rather eventful and exciting day and the morning after it would be like sinking deeper in a well in hell.

I learned to control my anger by channeling the anger and punishing myself emotionally since I did not want my anger to build into violence towards people who have wronged me in one way or another. In these cases, it was better me than them who suffer.

In all through that, I have made myself an asset to God, country and fellowmen. Never did I turn my back to those who needed help that I am capable of giving. Never did I fail to thank God for each new day and every breath that I take. As far as I know, I gave kindness whenever it was needed. I admit I have many bouts of anger but I have so far avoided physical violence to anybody as much as I can. In my mind, I only imagine the things that I would do to them if ever I let go of self-control. I have lived and loved all my life. But all my life I have also kept the demons inside me in check as best I could. Depression is not funny. It has no On/Off Switch. It is not cute and most of all it is not to be the subject of jokes. It has a debilitating effect. There are days when one finds it hard to function.

Joey De Leon may have apologized. Those who laughed with him are the true victims of mental illness. I never asked for an apology and never will. I will never ask for understanding. What I do ask is do not defend the likes of those who ridicule people with mental and emotional illnesses. Do not try to understand them. They are wicked and evil. They are the real ones who are sick. They have no cure. For those of us in the same boat, I will end with a quote from Voltaire, "What cannot be cured must be endured."

And Yes. Every Morning.

ooooo

10
Heroes - Several
August 29, 2016

Dr. Jose Rizal just got out of his clinic after a day of consultations. He was just waiting for the chance to get back to his hobby of online anthropological research on the difference of Filipinos and Europeans that his non-academic research that will eventually be published by a friend abroad named Blumetritt. As he was passing by Azcarraga, he saw two motorcycle guys riding in tandem gunning down a pedicab driver. Then a cardboard was tossed on the hapless victim. Being a doctor, he quickly rushed to the fallen man, the cardboard read "Huwag akong tularan. Pusher ako". Paying no heed to the sign, he saw that the man was beyond medical help with two gunshot wounds to the head and 5 to the chest.

Dr. Rizal then saw a woman running and then cradling the dead man to her chest. Dr. Rizal was moved because of the scene. His travel back to his home was with a disturbed conscience. All his education here and abroad was useless to save the man. He is active in the Silangan Lodge and other civic groups. He was instrumental in various medical missions and also reserved 1 day a month for free consultations to indigent families. His active participation in feeding programs for poor children every Saturday morning at the Barangay Hall has been going on for years.

Upon arriving home, he went inside his den, something was still bothering him. He turned on the TV and saw news of killings of alleged addicts and pushers on TV Patrol. The president was interviewed and that a statement that sacrifices must be made for peace and order. That human rights must take a back seat to the exigencies of fulfilling a campaign promise.

Dr. Rizal then turned off the tv and turned on his laptop and proceeded to open his current paper he wanted to finish drafting. He logged in to facebook and read the newsfeed. It also featured posts with pictures of those killed and the flame wars now a regular feature of facebook. He noted all the hate being thrown around by fb account holders with fictitious names and accounts.

Dr. Rizal posted his feelings. "I have devoted my life in curing people, helping them, giving them the chance in improving their lot. It was never easy. A lot of effort in giving them a chance to improve their lives and then the life is gone in a few seconds because of these roving vigilantes. In a few seconds, a comment was made. It told Dr. Jose Rizal that he was a protector of addicts and criminals. His sisters and mother must be raped.

Dr. Jose Rizal opened up a new file and started to write "Cardboard Justice".....

Emilio Jacinto rode the MRT going home from school. He was just 19 years old but he knew he must make a stand with regards to the killings. He wore an improvised cardboard sign that said "Lahat tayo pwedeng maging Pusher". There were stares as he was getting off the platform at Shaw Blvd. Station. Wanting to get some merienda at Shang Mall, he tried to enter the mall at its 5th level. The guard at the entrance told him to remove the cardboard sign he was wearing. Emilio insisted that he was not violating anything. He even showed his student ID and opened his backpack for inspection but the guard would not let him in without removing his cardboard sign. There were people in line that were waiting to be allowed in. When they saw and heard the discussion, someone shouted "tanggalin mo na kasi yan para makapasok na kami. Istorbo ka eh. Bakla!"

Emilio, noting the angry stares thrown his way just went down the MRT station stairs and took a ride going to Pasig. All the other passengers gave him dagger looks and it was a ride that seemed to last an eternity until he arrived at the Pasig Immaculate Conception Basilica. He got off and took a tricycle to his home. The tricycle driver seeing his sign asked if he was an activist or a drug addict.

Emilio got home and wrote his experiences in his blog. He used fb to chat with like minded friends and classmates. Apol Mabini, one of the older guys in the chatgroup then told them that he is in contact with a guy and they were already organizing. Apol told Emilio that the man who was organizing was a follower of Emilio's blog and requested that they meet up. Emilio agreed and Apol sent a different PM to the man who acknowledged the message.

"OK, sige meet tayo sa Starbucks Metrowalk 5:00 PM bukas." He typed on his laptop. Then he drew up another FB chat, "Dr. Rizal, bukas 5:00 pm tayo sa Starbucks Metrowalk, may bata ako, introduce sa iyo. We have already started to organize. Jun Luna and his brother Col. Tony Luna will also attend. There is restiveness now in the AFP and PNP". Andy Bonifacio then logged out.

ooooo

11
Heroes – Andres Bonifacio
September 4, 2016

    Andy Bonifacio was about to turn in for the night. He was just gazing from the window of his 2-storey house and watching the goings on of the street below him. His meeting with Apol Mabini, Emilio Jacinto and the Luna brothers the past week still resonated in his mind.

Andy was thinking of how things came to such a pass. He was born after the 1986 EDSA Revolution. It was when he was 5 years old that he knew what Martial Law was about. Actually, it was not directly. It was during the heat of the 1992 election campaign when his parents were campaigning for Sen. Jovito Salonga that he learned that the old man was a victim of the Plaza Miranda bombing. Up to then, Plaza Miranda was where Jollibee is located. It was there where they went after Sunday Mass at the Quiapo church. His grandparents took him there each Sunday. He asked how such a thing could happen in such a place. It was on a Sunday afternoon that his father, a supervisor at a shipping firm showed him pictures of EDSA 1986. He was told that a year later after that bombing, Martial Law was declared. That was the reason why they were campaigning for Salonga, for he was one of those who stood up against Martial Law. No matter if he was already frail, blind in one eye, deaf in one ear and missing several digits in his hands. His mother told Andy that there are men worth emulating and so he must study hard and be like Salonga. Andy had this quizzical look on his face when told of studying when he was only on his first grade in school.

The Knowledge of Good and Mostly Evil

Andy grew up being studious and also street smart. His first cognizance of the differences in social classes was when he was transferred to a private school for his high school education. He was not in agreement with it since he will leave behind his childhood friends in Juan Sumulong (John Forward) Elementary School. But his grandfather insisted since a retired educator himself, he saw the potential of Andy who excelled in the social sciences and mathematics at the same time. Also, having a proficiency in Pilipino and English at the same time. Andy remembered the rows and rows of books of his grandfather whenever he would visit them at Teachers Village in Quezon City. He would bring comics that he bought at National Book Store and bring them with him and asked his grandfather how to pronounce words and what they meant. In time he learned to read his grandfather's books himself.

Andy saw the differences between his childhood friends and his new classmates in the private school. Not only in their clothes and school supplies but also in their manners. These boys had a finesse about them and they were not all that rough and tumble like Boknoy and Junior Kalbo. Goldwyn and the other guys had nice, white and crisp polo shirts that never seemed to lose their creases even after the end of the school day. They even had pretty sisters who talked in English even when not in school.

Of course Andy would still hang out with Boknoy and Junior Kalbo and Lando on

Saturdays and Sundays when there were no school related activities. In fact, they would shout his name outside their gate during such mornings and they would ride their bikes all the way to Arranque and buy pigeon feed. They had collective pigeon coops that they managed to maintain and increase since 4th Grade. But on some Saturday evenings, Andy's world would change. His father would drive him to a soiree where he would mingle with girls from another school and He knew Muffy and Marina would never hang out with Boknoy and the others in his neighbourhood. Yes, Andy knew about drinks since he together with Boknoy and the gang would buy (bilog) and Mountain Dew on other Saturdays and drink behind the stage at the basketball court. In these soirees though, alcohol was strictly prohibited but Goldwyn and Caco would sneak in vodka (sapberry flavour) too.

As Andy went on to college, he got totally immersed with his studies and also exposed to the LFS. But the exigencies of his studies (he also enrolled in optional ROTC) took up most of his time. Junior Kalbo went to the home province of his father, Lando dropped out of school and now drove a tricycle and Boknoy was taken by his mother to the US.

During all these times, Andy would participate in election campaigns (local) because of family ties. He never experienced a time when there were no elections and the advent of first, cable TV and then the internet enabled him to get information as much as he wanted. It was here that he researched Martial Law. It was because of times when they had house guests and they talked about Mendiola and Welcome and Ayala. He never had any idea how it was to have no freedom, being born after EDSA.

But being a bank employee at a government financial institution, he also learned the real economy, what is unemployment and a stagnant agricultural sector since these were their clients in the bank. In fact, he saw what was needed for national development and learned to question the economic policies of the government.

This was then that Andy decided that he must take a more active part via groups that espoused a more economically sound policy. It was here that he came into contact not only with like minded people but also those with a whole new different perspective with regards to social and political policies.

Things came to a head when the elections resulted in a mere plurality elected president riding a wave of deep disenchantment for the policies of the last 30 years. Although trained in economics, finance and governance, Andy tried to wrestle with the phenomena that just happened. It was also the acrimonious campaign period that he realized the fissures in society and that a wave of EJKs were the norm in traditional media that he started to contact these persons that he got to know before. This was a time for organizing and trying to stave off the resulting firestorm that the country is headed. His meeting last week at Starbucks Metrowalk was a step towards that direction.

After finishing his cigarette , he turned to his TV which was kept on "mute".

Davao Night Market Bomber says the quotron of CNN Philippines. Andy told himself that this is going to be a mean season.

ooooo

12
Heroes – Emilio Jacinto
September 13, 2016

Emil Jacinto was just about to get a ride after his class. His meeting the last week kept him pondering on what to do next. He hoped that he will be able to have enough time to finish his 2 term papers and get a head start on his thesis. The cardboard sign he wore around his neck he no longer carried since he walked from Diliman to Cubao the other day. He was drenched to the bone when classes were suspended during mid-day. It was really hard getting a ride and so he walked to Cubao and rode a jeepney going to Rosario, Pasig. He heard that EDSA was at a standstill and he saw during his walk that EDSA was indeed one hue parking lot. His cardboard sign was soked and was turned into pulp by the time he reached Cubao. Such was his lot he told himself. He sent an sms to his mother that he will be late coming home and told of his travails. His mother was already preparing dinner and told him it would be Almondegas.

At the corner of EDSA and East Avenue, he saw his ROTC upperclassman. Greggy del Pilar ws popular on campus. Although, Emil thought of the hardships at the ROTC COCC he underwent under Greggy. Given the circumstances, Greggy smiled and told him to come over. He told Emil that since they were walking and already wet from the rain, Greggy would treat him at the nearby lugawan when they reach Kamuning.

"Emil, lugaw tayo, treat kita." Greggy said. Greggy was from Cainta, Rizal and he hoped to get a ride in Cubao too. "Hirap talaga ng sitwasyon natin. Akala ko mawawala na itong trapik after ng bagong president. Same old shit.". Emil was not wary. He know of the political stance of Greggy but he did not disclose that he was already in contact with those who opposed the new administration. Greggy respected Emil since he saw Emil as a fellow traveller and part of the Corps of Cadets. Greggy was also one of the bright stars in the university.

Emil and Greggy walked all the way to Cubao. In that one experience, they talked about a lot of things going on around. Although Greggy was the more martial of the two, Greggy respected Emil's concerns with regards to threats to freedom and human rights. "Akala ko nga OK na tayo eh. Kaya nga ako nag Advance ROTC para magkaroon ng training on how to protect the motherland if needed." "Mukhang sa iba ko magagamit" Greggy disclosed. "Bahala na" Emil retorted.

When they got a ride at Cubao, Emil said "sa tingin mo, magiging malala pa kaya?". Greggy smiled and said"di ko rn alam, mas matanda lang ako sa iyo ng isang taon, bakit ako tinanatanong mo?" and then the smiled turned into a laugh. "Sa kwento ng mga tito at tita ko, mas mahirap yung naranasan nila nung panahon ni Marcos". "Pero walang makasagot bakit pinayagan ng ilang taon na mag Martial Law?" Emil just mulled over the answer and then "Sa tingin ko di ako papaya na tumagal ang ganung sitwasyon, iba na panahon ngayon. Mas madali na communicatios dahil sa technology." Emil said. Greggy then answered "technology din ang ginamit ng mga nag elect sa gobyerno ngayon" "mukhang mahihirapan this time around." Iyan yung nasabi sa akin nung isa kong ka chat sa fb na nakaranas din ng Martial Law" "Minsan talaga di ko malaman kung seryoso o talagang may katok sa ulo yung si Budoy.". Emil again pondered on that since he also heard that from Apol Mabini.

Upon reaching Rosario, Emil got off. It was then that there was a crowd milling near Dr. Sixto Antonio avenue where he will get a ride going to Pasig. He had classmate there and he saw Rollie. "Umabot na dito talaga" Rollie said. There was a man lying on a pool of blood. Rollie said, "kilala ko yan, kapatid ni Bukol yan." Emil was about to ask when Rollie continued "Riding in tandem. Hindi talaga bubuhayin eh. Pito ang tama." Emil felt a shiver, not because he was still wet but a coldness born out of terror and fear. Walking home, he asked himself what can be done? It was not like all of this was a secret. It was being done in plain sight. Even official statistics have showed that close to 3,000 have already died. It was as if the whole country was giving in to bloodlust. Something must be done. He would try to chat about it with Andy Bonifacio.

He was online when he got home. Emil transmitted the picture via PM to Andy. Andy just told him, we are still organizing but it is good that this is documented. Do not post this on your timeline nor write about this in your blog. "We are going underground" Andy said. Emil just had this far away look. The Almondegas warmed his belly but not his heart.

ooooo

13

Heroes – Elias Santiago
September 19, 2016

    Elias Santiago or Ely looked left and right before going out the door of his house or abode or hole in the wall. It depends on one's perspective. The 8x4 dwelling is home to Ely. He shares it with his wife and child who is 3 years old. Ely just turned 21 last Saturday and he barely got to celebrate it until his brother, Ignacio came with 2 liters of Emperador Lite and lechon manok.

    At first, he did not want Ignacio to show up since Ignacio was also a small time pusher. But he was his only brother and his sister passed away 2 years ago because of complications with childbirth or Ely wanted to believe. He just do not want to listen to stories that his sister overdosed on shabu since she was already having contractions on her stomach and wanted the pain to go away.

Ely looked both ways again and took a step. It has only been a few weeks when many of his gang "surrendered" and went to the barangay hall. Oplan Tokhang has not reached their eskinita yet but somebody from the barangay went around with a list that showed names of drug addicts and small time pushers. Having found out that they had their names on the list prompted many of them to "surrender". Ely's name was not on that list. He avoided successfully taking shabu even though most of his friends were hooked on the stuff. He just did not like it, that's what he told himself. He was now on his way to the plaza area where he has this small stall that repaired cellphones and other gadgets.

He never had time to kiss Linda goodbye, she was out early being a laundrywoman and she took their child with her. Ely gave Rooney 2 Pochi as they went. He hoped to get some business by 11:30 a.m. buy lunch and go home and after that return to his repair stall after lunch and earn some more before buying their supper.

It was a hardscrabble life for him and his family. He got Linda pregnant when they were both 17 and just graduated from high school. Having a son gave him such a heavy responsibility that he was afraid to think 2 weeks in advance. He just worked, went home and played with his son. The regular drinking session with neighbors would come in twice a week and a brother who would drop by once a week was what occupied his time. He had a small TV set with cable connections (courtesy of neighborhood drug addicts who made the illegal connections) and a DVD player that he was able to buy from another drug addict who must have stolen it.

He was riding his BMX bike (a survivor of his transition from boyhood to manhood to parenthood all in a span of 1 year) when he saw SWAT vehicles going the opposite way. He knew he was too small a fry to be bothered and even if he did bother, they would just ignore somebody like him. The only attention he got was when the owner of the sari-sari store would remind him of what he owed the guy.

He arrived at the stall and removed the netting. Setting up his CPU and other tools took a whole of 5 minutes and he was open for business. Magno, the other stall owner who sold headphones, chargers and other gadgets sauntered up to him. "Pare, eto may 2 pang hopia. Merienda natin. Hoy Gemo, 2 gulaman, paki dala mo dito, dito ko na babayaran." Magno would do this almost every morning. He was thankful that the cellphone repair stall also generated business for him. It was symbiotic business relationship. "Nag inuman kami ni Ignacio kagabi. Di mo man lang ako inimbita nung birthday mo" Magno feigned hurt but he delivered it with a smile. "Biglaan lang naman yun, dumating si Ignacio may dalang empi at lechon manok. "OK lang yun, biro lang. Eto, hopia, happy birthday hahahaha!".

It was almost noon when Ely took up the contents of the box, he now had money for lunch. He bought 3 Okoy and 6 lumpiang shanghai and 3 orders of rice. As he was bicycling home, he was nearly sideswiped by the barangay ambulance. Hurrying home via the callejon, Linda with Rooney stopped him. She was in tears. "Ely, huwag ka muna umuwi, nag raid ang SWAT kanina pagkatapos mong umalis. Hinabol si Ignacio, dun na corner sa may kapilya, patay na."

Ely rushed to the kapilya, there was already a security cordon. "kapatid niya ako" he told one policeman. He saw Ignacio. Half his head was blown away and uncounted bullet holes riddled his body. Ely's knees buckled to the ground. He knew that his brother was a small time pusher. A small time pusher. But what he is seeing now is not a small time pusher. It was not even a pig slaughtered. A slaughtered pig does not look like that. His mind raced back when they were just children. Ignacio was always a big brother to him. Ignacio was the one who brought him to school and picked him up after school. It was Ignacio who came up with the money when his wife gave birth and it was Ignacio who spent for the baptism of Rooney. Ely knew that Ignacio was a pusher but Ely also knew that Ignacio was his brother. Ignacio did not deserve to be butchered like this.

Ely composed himself and went back to his stall. He will close early today. He will just wait until he has enough for dinner. He could not afford to wallow in despond. He had mouths to feed. Magno came up "Sorry Ely, kaibigan ko din naman si Ignacio." Magno looked down. "Parang tayo lang ang kayang patayin di ba?". Ely had this far away look. "Ely, may ipakikilala ako sa iyo. Hindi tama ang ginagawa eh. Para tayong mga ipis na pinupuksa". "Sige, ipakilala mo ako." Ely replied without even looking at Magno. Ely was gazing at the bell tower of the church and so much hated that the day is coming to an end.

ooooo

14

Heroes – PS Insp. Augusto Tirona
September 20, 2016

P/S Insp. Augusto Tirona was having a bad day. He was suffering from a headache brought about by a bad hangover. He and 3 of his men had 3 liters of Emperador the previous day. It started early enough at around 2 in the afternoon but it dragged on until 10:00 p.m. His men, Lito and another one "Bulik" and Julian were in the PCP drinking because of domestic troubles of Capt. Tirona. The alternating hot sun and short but sharp rains all throughout the morning tested Tirona's nerves. Although he and his men were not I the frontlines, they were still ordered to deploy behind the Civil Disturbance Control phalanx that faced the demonstrators.

Tirona's men were armed unlike the CDC before them. The rallyists were able to barricade themselves behind the 10-wheeler truck that served as their stage earlier in their morning program. It was not supposed to be this way since earlier orders from Gen. Kamagong was for the policy of maximum tolerance. They though they outsmarted the demonstrators. Although the demonstrators sat behind the students who lay down on the road leading to the Libingan ng mga Bayani, their plan was to fly in the body of ex-President Marcos. But the organizers of the demonstrators also had contingencies. When the helicopter was approaching, a barrage of fireworks were lighted, dozens of rockets filled the air and the helicopter could not safely approach. It turned out that the 10-wheeler truck not only brought the stage and sound systems but also brought with it face masks, water, the fireworks along with enough food to last for days. It also brought a generator that powered laptops, cellphones and gadgets that brought streaming video to the internet. After 3 attempts the helicopter could not loiter anymore and would have to return to Villamor Air Base. The demonstrators felt victory at hand.

Also, employees from Ayala went down from their offices and are now marching down McKinley Road. Employees from Ortigas Business Center were also now marching down C5 and were already at Bagong Ilog, Pasig. The Police and the AFP never had any such contingencies. Radio reports of clashes between police and demonstrators coming from Quezon City were being fed them and the stopline was in

Cubao where those in Araneta Center were attempting to outflank the blocking force at EDSA corner Aurora. There can be had no reinforcements from Crame or Aguinaldo since a large part is already in Cubao and another contingent was blocking Shaw Blvd because of demonstrators coming from Mandaluyong and Manila.

The adjacent provincial commands had to send augmentation forces to surround Malacanang. It would be hours before more units can be poured in from Rizal and Bulacan. A day at least from Quezon Province and Bicol commands. It took them by surprise since all they expected was resistance from the demonstrators already at the BGC.

Tirona was given the order to move forward since the CDC was already advancing towards the demonstrators. Then several teargas launchers were fired against the rally line. But instead of dispersing, the rallyers poured water over their eyes and face marks. Those lying down were also doused with water, thus the teargas was neutralized. The Amihan wind also blew the teargas towards the police line and greatly degraded the operations. Not all the policemen and soldiers were issued gas masks.

But the CDC reached the demonstrators lying down on the road. The impact was psychological. It was one thing to use truncheons on standing demonstrators. It was different beating down on students who were lying down.

Emilio and Gregorio were the one's who were sitting down in front of the students lying down. They were part of the UP contingent. Those lying down were students from UST and Ateneo. The troopers cannot beat them down but they tried pulling them up and carrying them but the students held on to each other's hands and arms. They were locked in a human mesh. No matter how hard they tried, it was useless. The CDC was faltering. Tirona had his men with guns firing rubber bullets come forward. When the CDC retreated in frustration, Tirona ordered a volley. The first rank of those sitting down crumpled. Emilio was hit on the chest and he crumpled over. Gregorio carried him to the back and other students took their place. Again Tirona ordered a volley and the front line of the students went down, but again others took their place.

Tirona was already frustrated, a third volley was ordered with the same results. Students already had bloody heads and faces. Tirona then stepped on the bodies of the students lying down. He did not care if it was a face or a stomach or a leg. A priest the stood up and told him that it was enough. Then a nun implored him to cease the volley of rubber bullets. More than 1 hundred students were bleeding behind them.

Gregorio took Emiio to the aid station. Dr. Jose Rizal together with volunteer nurses and doctors were treating the casualties and more were coming. Dr. Jose Rizal then went towards the frontlines because of the continuous flow of casualties. He was wearing his white coat and just following the line of litter-bearers who came streaming to the aid station. When he got to the from, he saw the final volley of rubber bullets and his hands turned white with rage upon seeing the students being mown down.

But the students and other demonstrators would not back down. They started to sing Lupang Hinirang which was commenced by a lone UP Music Conservatory student. It was such a stirring voice that upon the second stanza, all the others sang together with her.

Tirona was blocked by the priest and nun. He could not hear what they were saying since the national anthem was being sang around them. Tirona took out his 9mm Beretta and pointed it at the priest to order them to stop. The priest just stood there. The nun seeing the gun tried to yank Tirona's arm. Tirona, confused, having a bad headache and the loudness of the song pulled the trigger. The priest crumpled and fell down, the nun draped her body over another student. Tirona said "Putang ina ninyo, tumigil na kayo!", But the students only sang louder, He pointed his gun towards the head of another student sitting down. It was Gregorio, the nun dived over Gregorio, the gun went off and the bullet hit the nun.

Dr. Rizal was running towards Tirona but other policemen went to Tirona and carried him off toward their lines. Dr. Rizal knelt with tears running down his cheeks. The priest was dead and the nun had a gunshot wound on her side. Gregorio was trying to stanch the blood on the nun. Dr. Rizal took the puls of the priest as the song ended at "Ang Mamatay ng Dahil sa iyo…….."

Events were now being livestreamed over the internet. Pictures were being posted realtime on facebook. The demonstrators even had drones flying of the carnage. The world saw what was happening.

At the same time, Andy Bonifacio was with a group inside vans that were heading to Sampaloc…

Ooooo

15
Heroes – Apolinario Mabini
Dateline, 2017

Apol Mabini was just waiting by the kiosk across the PLDT Office at Sampaloc, Manila. Classes were suspended by noon. News has been going around on what happened at the Libingan ng mga Bayani and the employees of Ayala and Ortigas business districts. Already, there were students and other protesters at Mendiola. They had returned after being dispersed by Civil Disturbance Control units earlier in the morning. What led to the return bout was the appearance of pro-government mob who cornered a group of students isolated near Tandem. A group of students then threw rocks at them and they chased the students all the way to Morayta little knowing that a bigger group was waiting for them and ambushed them sealing both ends of Morayta. The pro-government mob were themselves cut off and were beaten up until none were left standing. There was no police to break up the fracas since most police were concentrated on Mendiola Bridge.

Lacson Avenue was already being filled with traffic. Welcome Rotonda was closed by the police since there was a contingent of students marching from UP, Ateneo and Miriam College. News travels fast in this age of the internet. Apol was lighting his third cigarette when 3 vans arrived. He saw Andy Bonifacio alighting from one and several people also disembarked. It was the signal for those also waiting in the area. They converged on the PLDT Office. Security guards were taken by surprise and a group managed to enter the building. Andy told Apol that this was strategic. They have to keep the international communications gateway open. PLDT must not be shut down. The group then proceeded to the Tower area and convinced the engineers to remain calm. Following the vans was a truck that brought in water, food and other supplies. The protesters were digging in.

Three police cars arrived but by that time, those manning the barricades were almost 2 thousand strong, mainly Civil Society groups and students from nearby UST. Andy let the

Civil Society negotiators deal with the police. He was communicating via the new FB Messaging that included encryption. He was talking to his brother Proxy who at that time was at the Meralco Substation with other protesters. There would be no brownouts in the area. They sealed off   the   substation.

Andy was on the line again with Syano Jaena who was at Ayala Boulevard. Syano was telling him that the entire Ayala Golden Mile was emptied out of employees and the tail end was at Mckinley Road proceeding to BGC. A group of protesters with nuns from Assumption and students from the Ateneo Business Schools were already manning the barricades at the corner of EDSA and Ayala and another group manned by Don Bosco brothers and students were barricading Ayala corner Buendia.

Syano Jaena was also online and saw the drone footage realtime at the Libingan ng mga Bayani. An Assumption Sister was also watching and tears were running down her cheeks when viewing the carnage at the LmnB. Such ruthless barbarity but the barricade was holding. Syano tried to call Dr. Jose Rizal on the encrypted FB PM but got no answer. The video showed that the teargas was clearing up and the police and military have taken a step back.

Back in Espana, Apol was manning the front line of the barricades together with students from UST. One of his law students was pointing at something. When he looked towards the area, he saw several SUVs and Pick-up trucks disembarking men. The vehicles prominently had DDS stickers on their sides. "Ah, Digong Duterte Supporters" he said to himself. This was expected since police and military units were already stretched, it was just a matter of time that such hoods will show up to augment the regular police and military.

These men charged the barricades and they had pistols out. A UST bother tried to block them but they shot him in the head. Guns spewed fire towards the protesters and a dozen fell down. Nobody ran away, in fact, more reinforced the frontlines. Stones and Molotov cocktails were thrown towards the group of gunmen. Five were immolated at once. A foodcart became part of the barricade. Five gunmen fired at the barricades and a bullet ricocheted and hit Apol at the back. He was attended to by a student and dragged towards the back.

Apol was in distress, not because of the attack but because he could not feel his legs.

Ooooo

16
Christmas Full Circle
Dateline, Dec. 20, 2017

5 more days until Christmas. For me, no matter the circumstances I find myself during this time of the year, I find it as the Real Season of Hope. It is not that I am waiting for miracles, like a Mercedes Benz (which I did have 7 years ago but no longer have) or a mansion or a trip to Europe. It is about having another Christmas by the grace of the Lord above.

In my lifetime which is 52 years, there were unfortunate circumstances in all those 52 Christmases past. But that did not mean that that Christmas was bad. In fact, those can be counted as among the best Christmases that I ever had.

It was not because I have so many gifts, lots of money or even having that rare wine that I first tasted when I was working at the palace more than a decade ago. It was Christmases that I learned to know what it really meant when I look back now.

That Christmas Eve in 1973 where we spent it at the Police Headquarters, where our Noche Buena was pansit and unlimited coffee made by other policemen. Papa was having a hard time at work then. But we were there as a family. No other Christmas like when the whole family is complete even in a Police Headquarters.

There was the Christmas Eve that we spent in a hospital ward where Mama lay terminally ill but praying and hoping for a miracle. The miracle did not come but God saw to it that we be all together that Christmas eve. Our last time as a complete family. I consider that last Christmas together as a gift from God. That was His gift to us. He gave us Christmas.

There was that Christmas Eve that my house burned down. But even then, the Lord gave me a Christmas. Just as long as we get Christmas.

Of course we remember the happy Christmases when we were children and even up to now. The bonuses and gifts.

It has come full circle for me now. Happiness is not Joy. Joy is that something that is inside each one of us, especially during this season. That whatever challenges and adversities we face, that despite what our efforts to have an ideal Christmas falls short, we know that God gave us hope and that better things are in store for all of us in the future.

The first Christmas was not the Boom Times of the economy. It was a time when the world needed hope. When Good News was direly needed. It arrived in a manger. In an animal shed.

No matter the circumstances, no matter the uncertainties, we are where God wants us to be. This is the perfect place for us now because God planned all of it.

The only condition then was that It Came Upon A Midnight Clear.

Ooooo

17

Living on the Edge
Dateline, Dec. 20, 2017

(Quote) Matthew 14:22-33
Jesus Walks on the Water

22 Immediately Jesus made the disciples get into the boat and go on ahead of him to the other side, while he dismissed the crowd.

23 After he had dismissed them, he went up on a mountainside by himself to pray. Later that night, he was there alone,

24 and the boat was already a considerable distance from land, buffeted by the waves because the wind was against it.

25 Shortly before dawn Jesus went out to them, walking on the lake.

26 When the disciples saw him walking on the lake, they were terrified. "It's a ghost," they said, and cried out in fear.

27 But Jesus immediately said to them: "Take courage! It is I. Don't be afraid."

28 "Lord, if it's you," Peter replied, "tell me to come to you on the water."

29 "Come," he said. Then Peter got down out of the boat, walked on the water and came toward Jesus.
30 But when he saw the wind, he was afraid and, beginning to sink, cried out, "Lord, save me!"

31 Immediately Jesus reached out his hand and caught him. "You of little faith," he said, "why did you doubt?"

32 And when they climbed into the boat, the wind died down.

33 Then those who were in the boat worshiped him, saying, "Truly you are the Son of God."

The above passages have been a staple of the "miracles" of Christ. But the miracle was not done because of only showing off the powers of the Lord. It was done to show what it means to walk with Christ and also for us to know how to walk with the Lord.

Life is like what was happening to that boat. It was being buffeted by waves and the wind. It was dark and the boat was being tossed about. Surely, nobody of sound mind would want to go out of the boat in such a situation.

Today, we are in the same situation. As my Tatay (Grandfather) would tell me decade ago, the world is in a state of flux. Everything is uncertain. The political situation is uncertain. The economy both of the country and the world is uncertain. Our personal finances are uncertain. Our relationships with our families, friends, bosses, co-workers and even romantic relations are uncertain.

In the midst of that, we have done everything we could to shield ourselves, and pur loved ones from all the uncertainties and the fear generated by these uncertainties. We try to have a modicum of security and protect our own little corner at great personal cost. Sometimes it will take a great amount of compromises to build even a flimsy fence around us. Then we call it peace and a haven. But every howl of the wind and the smash of waves shakes us and makes us fearful and afraid. It disrupts at even at the most subtle vibration that we feel. It is living in insecurity.

But God does not want us to live that way. He wants us to be happy in living our lives, to find joy in His creation.

Peter wanted that. That is why he called out and went over the ramparts of the boat. Peter did not want to live with fear and insecurity on a boat that is being rocked by waves. Peter did not want to have limited visibility in the middle of darkness. He saw the Lord walking on water and he wanted to be with the Lord.

But again, the wind howled and Peter felt afraid. He started to sink. But true to his faith, Peter cried out "Lord save me." And he was saved from sinking. It means that although we have taken faith of Christ does not mean we will not have problems and troubles anymore. The Lord reached out and held Peter's hand. That is the beauty of it. We will have problems and troubles still. Our harms may not be able to reach the Lord but the Lord's arms can reach us everywhere we may be. All we have to do is have faith and ask the Lord to save us and the Lord always does.

The real reason for this is that we may have troubles and problems today and plenty of them will come. The difference is we have the Lord walking with us and we will never sink as long as we hold His hand. All those who were left on the boat did not have enough faith and belief to step out of their comfort zones and that is why there were still afraid during that time. They must have felt Peter to be a fool to step out of the boat and go into the big waves, the howling winds and the darkness. But the Lord proved them wrong.

We profess to have faith but the next step is to get out of the boat and have the faith tested by all sorts of challenges and adversities. As long as we hold on to the Lord, we will never sink. That is what God wants for us, to live in security and joy for by doing that we will also give joy to God.

If we are in the middle of adversity, when the day seems the darkest, that is where God wants us to be. He placed us there because that is where we will find His hand and hold on to them with courage and   perseverance.

18
Today is my birthday.
Dec. 18, 2017

I will greet you all this time around. To all of those who are part of my life, my brother and sisters, my nieces and nephews, my uncles and aunts, cousins. To all my friends whom I have known from childhood, grade school, high school, college and in the course of my professional life up to today. To neighbors, team mates and colleagues who have taught me all that I know. To all the people whom I have interacted with that included teachers and professors. I mention those who have also served as mentors, even former and present bosses at work that have taught me my life skills today. I greet all my brothers and sisters in the faith, never shall we be alone for God is with us always. Greetings to the Special Interest Groups that I belong to, from the political to the Geek Sites and Groups. The Meek and the Geek shall inherit the earth.

Of course, to all past loves. Please forgive me for not mentioning your names Hahahahaha. No rancor or bitterness. I still love all of you and you remain in my heart.

To all of you, thank you very much. It has been 52 years and I have no regrets. The best part of the journey is getting to know all of you. You are all my treasures. I will always be grateful.

I started my day by going to the nearest church where I live. I am a Protestant but the nearest church is Roman Catholic. But God goes to where one seeks Him. I just gave thanks for everything and asked for nothing. I also went to the ossuary where the remains of Mama and Papa are relinquished. I prayed to God to convey to them how we are very thankful for them, how we miss them and how our love for them has never faded.

I gifted myself by having free lugaw meals be given to the street children, the beggars and the destitute courtesy of Alex Lugawan. Perhaps, God willing, it will be steak dinner for them next year.

Again, I send my greetings and felicitations to all of you. Thank you very much!

19
Every Morning
Dateline, October 6, 2017

*"The real hopeless victims of mental
illness are to be found among those who appear
to be most normal. "Many of them are normal
because they are so well adjusted to our mode
of existence, because their human voice has
been silenced so early in their lives, that they do
not even struggle or suffer or develop symptoms
as the neurotic does." They are normal not in
what may be called the absolute sense of the
word; they are normal only in relation to a
profoundly abnormal society. Their perfect
adjustment to that abnormal society is a
measure of their mental sickness. These millions
of abnormally normal people, living without fuss
in a society to which, if they were fully human
beings, they ought not to be adjusted."*

Jonathan Edwards J. Olabre   91

The Knowledge of Good and Mostly Evil

— Aldous Huxley, Brave New World
Revisited

"Tralala, tweedlededeedee it gives me a thrill, to wake up in the morning and hear the mockingbirds trill..." I heard that song when I was very young. It was being played on the radio when my grandparents were listening while having breakfast. With Milo and pan de sal with spiced ham it made my morning. Those days are gone.

I have had that feeling of an attack from an unexpected source since Grade 5. I felt it at school. I have classmates and teachers who I remember so well and never was I a victim of bullying. It was just the usual roughhousing in an all-boys school ran by priests. The stern teachers were strict but nurturing. At home, it was ideal as can be under any circumstances. A tall, providing father, a caring and kind mother, solicitous sisters, a beloved little brother and loving grandparents were the environment. I have friends in the neighborhood and their parents were also friends of my parents.

But even though I did good in school, those mornings were started with feelings of dread that I cannot understand why there was that feeling. I buried myself in books and biking. The feeling never went away though. In fact, it went to a point where I did not want good things to happen because I knew bad things will happen just to take away happiness.

The Knowledge of Good and Mostly Evil

Such was the state of things that I thought was normal even in high school. I learned to deal with it, never expected anything happy to happen or never wanted it to happen since there will come a day of gloom to take it all away.

With the way things went in the world, I thought it was normal. I thought it was just the way the world is. But I remember days when I was paralyzed by it. Days when I did not want to go to school or days I did not want to go to work even though I was doing good than many.

In college, the day started with Valium 10 that was supplied by a childhood friend because we thought it was cool and after the 1st class, my college buddy who is my lifelong best friend until now would tell me to start drinking Rhum Coke. He would have this 1 liter bottle of Coke which was half filled with Tanduay and of course the guards in the school thought it was only Coke. We studied and passed subjects and even got high grades in Physics at that. It was a coping mechanism. The College Guidance Counselor and the Office of Student Affairs identified me and my buddy and subjected us to a psycho test. It turned out that we were both neurotic and we laughed at it. They said they wanted us to take the test because we looked "weird." Years later I saw the former Director of the Office of Student Affairs and he told my boss (I was already working for the palace then) that I was one of the leaders of the "counter-culture" during college.

But that was after I was subjected to psychiatric care. I was diagnosed with clinical depression. My former boss tricked me into going to a psychiatric clinic because I was really spaced out. I was good at work, in fact, I was excelling at work. But by then, after work, my boss and I would go out for drinks and I can consume 20 bottles of beer without getting drunk. My former boss was worried and it turned out that the depressant in alcohol cannot go down to the level of depression that my system was already in. My system was already depressed. I was given medications and counseling. Eventually, I pulled back from the brink. But it never really went away.

Such that every morning, I would wonder why I am still alive and I have to explain and rationalize to myself that I have to live for that day. Every sunset that I see, I would have to explain to myself why I should not also end it that time.

I may be in Megamall and yet feel alone. I may be at the grand lobby of a hotel during a meeting and I would see everything spinning around me. Then it would be an anxiety attack and I would break out in cold sweat, shiver, tremble and feel like throwing up. It gets worse if I have had a rather eventful and exciting day and the morning after it would be like sinking deeper in a well in hell.

I learned to control my anger by channeling the anger and punishing myself emotionally since I did not want my anger to build into violence towards people who have wronged me in one way or another. In these cases, it was better me than them who suffer.

In all through that, I have made myself an asset to God, country and fellowmen. Never did I turn my back to those who needed help that I am capable of giving. Never did I fail to thank God for each new day and every breath that I take. As far as I know, I gave kindness whenever it was needed. I admit I have many bouts of anger but I have so far avoided physical violence to anybody as much as I can. In my mind, I only imagine the things that I would do to them if ever I let go of self-control. I have lived and loved all my life. But all my life I have also kept the demons inside me in check as best I could. Depression is not funny. It has no On/Off Switch. It is not cute and most of all it is not to be the subject of jokes. It has a debilitating effect. There are days when one finds it hard to function.

Joey De Leon may have apologized. Those who laughed with him are the true victims of mental illness. I never asked for an apology and never will. I will never ask for understanding. What I do ask is do not defend the likes of those who ridicule people with mental and emotional illnesses. Do not try to understand them. They are wicked and evil. They are the real ones who are sick. They have no cure. For those of us in the same boat, I will end with a quote from Voltaire, "What cannot be cured must be endured."

And Yes. Every Morning.

20
7 Years after that Christmas
Dateline, Dec. 20, 2017

Having woken up early on a morning this close to Christmas, I was still dwelling on thoughts after my morning quiet time and prayers. I was wondering what happened to those 2 boys that I met 7 years ago. It was Christmas Eve and I went out to buy cigarettes after cooking and preparing the table for Noche Buena. I saw 2 boys there at the store. They were drinking a bottle of Coke and eating Chippy. I asked them what they were doing still out so close to midnight. I asked them what their families were doing at this time of night. I was expecting that they would answer that their families would be preparing for Noche Buena. They both answered that their families were already asleep. It turned out that the Coke and Chippy were their Noche Buena. I asked how come that was the case. One boy answered that they do not have money and that his father was in jail. I told them to just stay put, I went inside. I made ham sandwiches and brought out a of bowl of macaroni salad that I just made. I brought it out and made them eat. They went home happy after that. I never saw them again.

Having finished on that thought, I went out to buy pan de sal. It turned out that there were a few of us standing in line because the pan de sal was still in the oven. I observed those were with me. There were 2 girls about 9 or ten years of age, a maid buying for her masters, a guy on a motorcycle and an old woman with a little girl. As usual, made up stories in my mind about people that were with me. Just little stories. The 2 girls were inutusan lang. The maid doing her duties. The guy going to buy breakfast for his family. The old woman was called lola by the girl.

Then, the pan de sal got baked and were being handed out to us. I saw the lola handing out 10 pesos, about 5 pieces worth of the now incredible shrinking pan de sal. Then I heard her say, sige kumain ka na. It turned out that 10 pesos worth of pan de sal constituted breakfast for her apo. I saw the look in the eyes of the lola. It was as if she was apologizing to her granddaughter that it was all she could afford. "Pasensiya ka na." was written all over her eyes.

As I was going home, I imagined how many cases like that is happening at that very minute, how the circumstances were being replicated while the morning light was just peeking. And such things happening this close to Christmas. I know it happens and such has been the case for centuries. But as I was passed by those who attended simbang gabi, I wondered how many of them prayed for the lola and her apo. I hope they were included in their prayers.

I am making sure that those 2 boys from seven years ago, that lola and little girl will be there. A prayer for all those who are in need and dire straights. Of lonely Filipinos on far away lands yearning for a Christmas at home. My prayers include those who are ill and infirm. Those who cannot see the lights and hear the carols. My prayers will be with them this coming Christmas. Because I know there also those who pray for me even without me knowing it, without me asking for it. That Christmas will mean that they are not alone.

21
Why I Publish/Reprint Books

**Tatay Jobo Blizes
Self-Publisher**

Writings are timeless and they act as mirrors to history. I publish writings as they remain relevant anytime. I have seen a lot of good writings in the internet, in magazines and newspapers. But most writers have only one or two articles and therefore not enough material to be published as a book. And yet, many of them need to be published or archived. There are also writers who write a lot but never publish them. There are also old books with no more prints available. The solution is to publish/reprint.

I do this for free because of the print-books-on-demand (POD) system, but the printed or hardcopy is not free

The printed book will always be there among your collections or libraries. Not all use the internet. The internet access has its technical problems. I can produce fiction, non-fiction, in color also.

My booklist can be seen at http://tinyurl.com/mj76ccq (copy and paste)

Permission had been granted by the author/ authors to print their books under my free self-publishing service. They own copyrights to their works.

Interested reader may request free reading of any of my books, articles or essays via online reading or ebook. Just email me.

Thank you.